Wally
AND THE SWEET MOUNTAIN CANDY FACTORY
Activity Book

THIS BOOK BELONGS TO:
_____

ABOUT ME:

I AM _____ YEARS OLD.

MY BIRTHDAY IS _____.

I LIVE IN _____.

THIS IS WHAT I LOOK LIKE:

Cover, layout and illustrations by Pencil Master Studio

©2021 Meghan Christensen

All rights reserved. No part of this book may be reproduced in any form or by any means, electronic or mechanical, including photocopy, recording, scanning, or any information storage and retrieval system, without permission in writing from the copyright holder.

Help Benji to the Candy!

Good Luck Wally!

Draw Wally's neighborhood and friends cheering him on for his first day of work at Sweet Mountain Candy Factory.

I Spy

Find It

Color the hidden objects in the picture.

Word Search

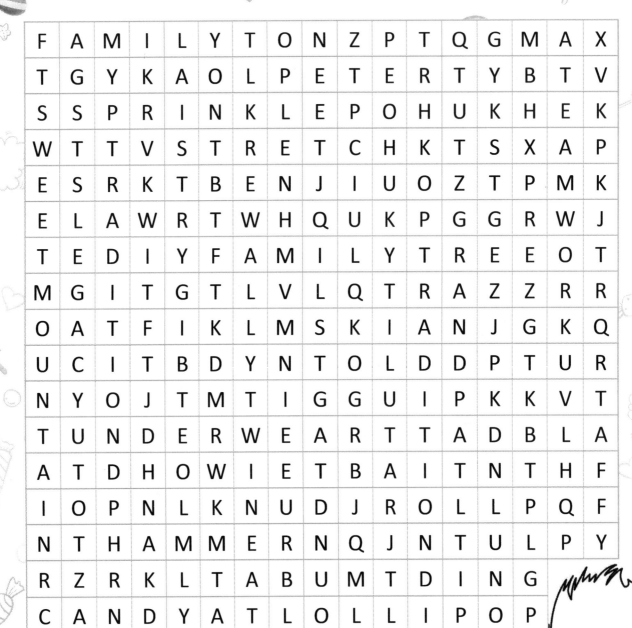

F	A	M	I	L	Y	T	O	N	Z	P	T	Q	G	M	A	X
T	G	Y	K	A	O	L	P	E	T	E	R	T	Y	B	T	V
S	S	P	R	I	N	K	L	E	P	O	H	U	K	H	E	K
W	T	T	V	S	T	R	E	T	C	H	K	T	S	X	A	P
E	S	R	K	T	B	E	N	J	I	U	O	Z	T	P	M	K
E	L	A	W	R	T	W	H	Q	U	K	P	G	G	R	W	J
T	E	D	I	Y	F	A	M	I	L	Y	T	R	E	E	O	T
M	G	I	T	G	T	L	V	L	Q	T	R	A	Z	Z	R	R
O	A	T	F	I	K	L	M	S	K	I	A	N	J	G	K	Q
U	C	I	T	B	D	Y	N	T	O	L	D	D	P	T	U	R
N	Y	O	J	T	M	T	I	G	G	U	I	P	K	K	V	T
T	U	N	D	E	R	W	E	A	R	T	T	A	D	B	L	A
A	T	D	H	O	W	I	E	T	B	A	I	T	N	T	H	F
I	O	P	N	L	K	N	U	D	J	R	O	L	L	P	Q	F
N	T	H	A	M	M	E	R	N	Q	J	N	T	U	L	P	Y
R	Z	R	K	L	T	A	B	U	M	T	D	I	N	G		
C	A	N	D	Y	A	T	L	O	L	L	I	P	O	P		

Candy
Family
Legacy
Family Tree
Tradition
Wally
Tigg
Max

Peter
Benji
Grandpa
Sweet Mountain
Howie
Razz
Lollipop
Taffy

Ski
Teamwork
Sprinkle
Stretch
Roll
Hammer
Underwear
Ding

Wally's on His Way!

Help Wally get to work at the Sweet Mountain Candy Factory!

Let's Decorate Candy!

Add your own stripes, polka dots, and zig-zags! Color each piece to look different and unique, just like you!

Dot to Dot

Draw from 1 to 89 to create a picture.

Welcome to the Candy Store!
Draw some delicious candy in the window.

Dress Wally for a Day in the Snow!
Color, cut, and glue the winter clothes on Wally.

Dress Wally for His Work Day!
Color, cut, and glue the Sweet Mountain uniform on Wally.

Become a Candy Maker!

Put on your candy making hat, it's time to make some candy!

Cut out the hat pieces and glue together to form a headband. Wear when making candy in your own kitchen!

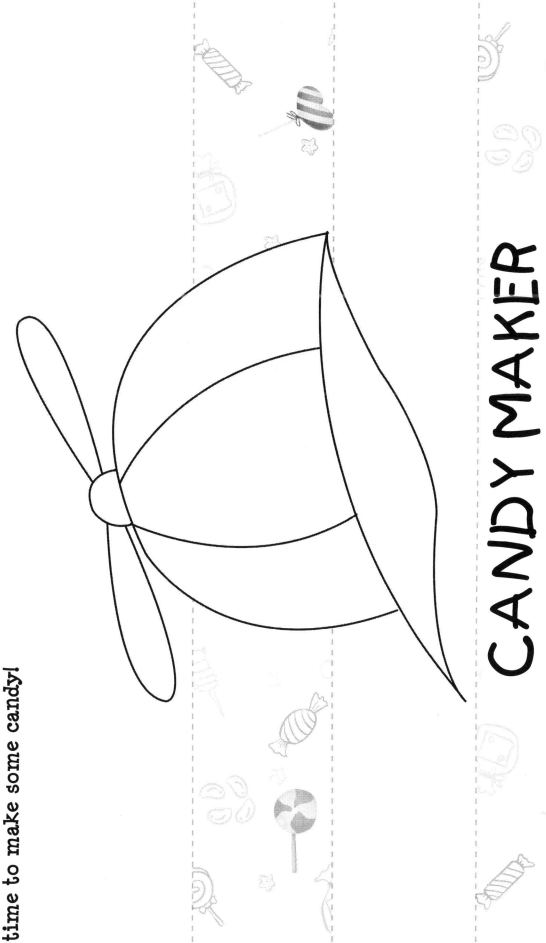

CANDY MAKER

Let's Play!
Put on your own puppet show!

Color and cut out Wally and his friends. (Be careful not to cut off the side tabs!) Use the tabs to make rings for your fingers.

Don't Eat Benji!

1. Place a candy on each square. **2.** Send one person out of the room. **3.** Remaining players choose a square to be "Benji". **4.** The person who left comes back. (Shh don't tell them which square is "Benji") **5.** The person touches (or eats!) one piece of candy at a time, trying NOT to pick the one designated as "Benji". **6.** There is no talking until the secretly chosen "Benji" square is touched, then all shout, "Don't eat Benji!!" Their turn is over. **7.** Refill the board, pick a new person to leave the room, and a new "Benji" square. **8.** Whoever picks the most candy before finding "Benji", wins!

Count and Color
How many can you find?

Count and Color

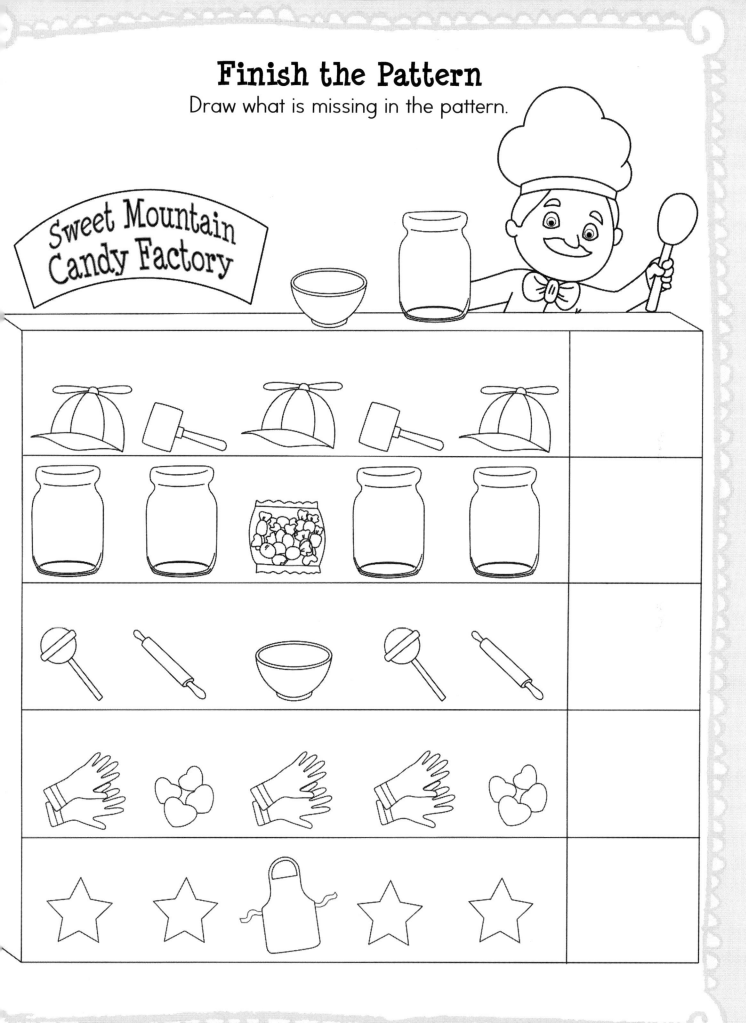

Candy Counter

Count the candy in each jar.

Color by Letter

A - Purple • E - Blue • I - Orange • O - Red • U - Green

Spot the Difference
Can you find the 10 Differences?

How Do You Feel?

Finish each face by drawing the emotions.

I'm happy

I'm surprised

I'm sad

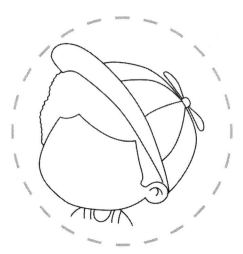

I'm sleepy

I'm silly

I'm angry

Let's Do Our Hair!

Draw on the correct hairstyle for Wally and his friends.

WALLY

BENJI

SIMIE

PETER

TIGG

How to Draw Wally

My Family

Draw a picture of your family doing your favorite activity together.

My family is special to me because:

_____

_____

_____

If I Had a Candy Factory...

This is what my candy factory would look like:

This is what my work uniform would look like:

This is what flavors I would have:

_____

_____

_____

_____

Bookmarks

Color and cut out the 4 bookmarks. Laminate for a sturdier version.

Surprise a Friend!

Color, cut out the top rectangle, fold on the dotted line, and glue together where marked. Slide a favorite candy inside. Leave your surprise on your friend's pillow, doorstep, or favorite spot!

Let's Play!
Grab a buddy and play Tic-Tac-Toe together!

Decode the Secret Message.

Fill in the blanks with the letter that matches each picture to reveal the message.

F A M I L Y

M A K E S   L I F E

S W E E T

🍬	F	🌲	L	⛷	S	
🎁	K	🔨	A	🥖	O	
🧢	T	👕	I	❄	Y	
🥞	M	🍭	W	🍴	E	

Let's Go Skiing!

Color and cut out each of the characters. Glue popsicle sticks to their feet to become skis and toothpicks in their hands as poles. Hit the slopes!

My Family Tree

Write the names, draw, or glue a picture of each of your family members in their correct spots.

"This is me!"

Wally is Excited to Be at Sweet Mountain Candy Factory!

What do you get excited about?

_____

Wally Loves to Ski!

Cut along the dotted lines and roll, each strip from the bottom to the top, onto a pencil. Slide the pencil out of the strip and see the snow mounds come to life!

How to Make Sweet Mountain Candy!

Cut out the steps and glue them in the correct order to make candy at the Sweet Mountain Candy Factory.

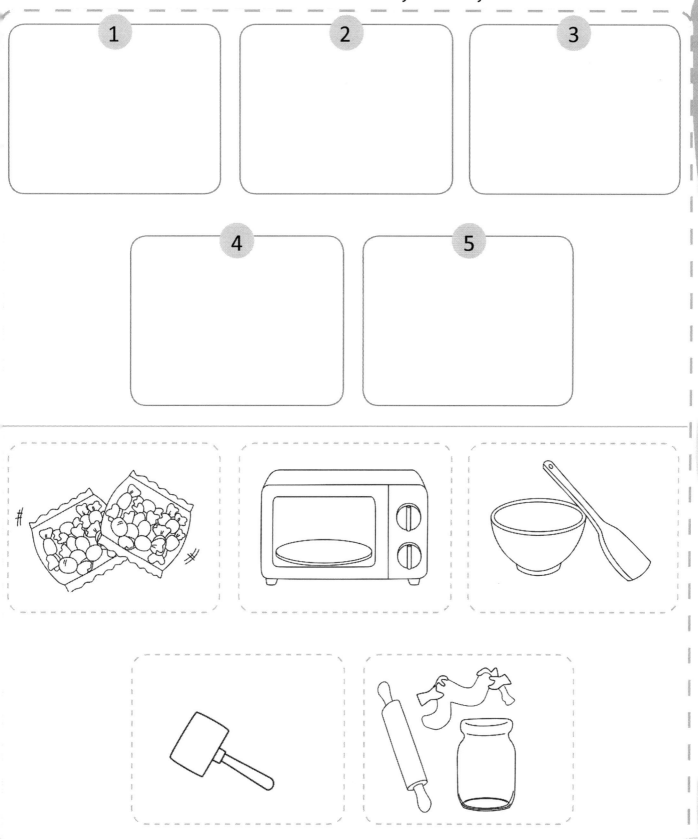

Stretch, Roll, and Sprinkle!

Do you remember Wally's friend's names?

_____   _____

_____   _____

Package and Mail the Candy for You to Eat! Yum!

What is your favorite candy?

_____

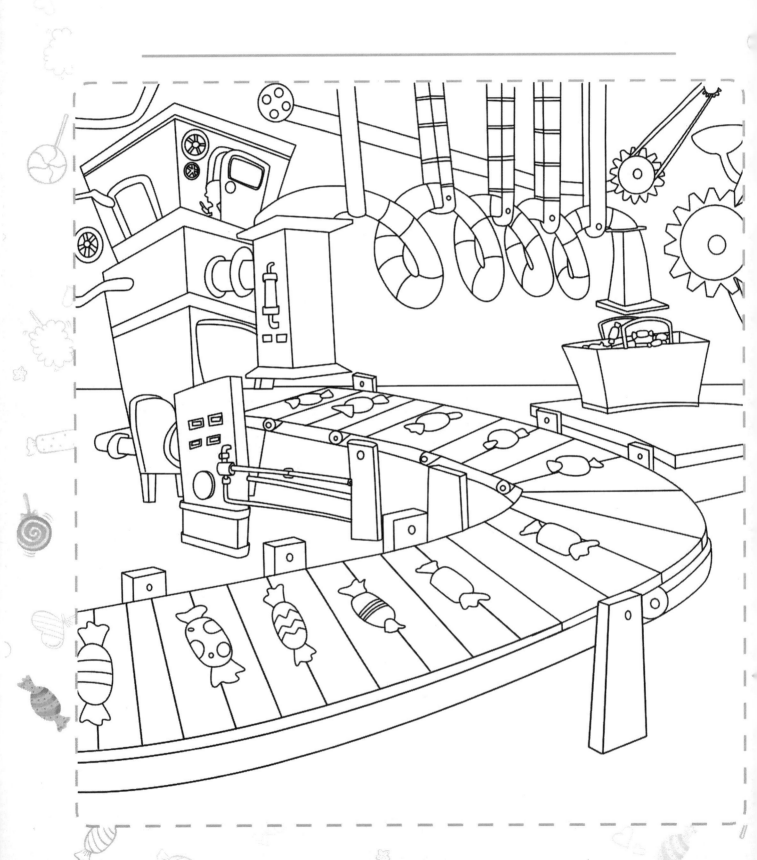

Oh No! Benji Got Caught on the Speed Switch!

How would you help Benji down? Circle the option you would choose.

You Are SUPER!

What makes you awesome?

_____

Wally and Benji are Best Buddies.

Do you have a best buddy? What is their name?

_____

Today Is Wally's First Day of Work at His Family's Sweet Mountain Candy Factory!

What do your family members do for work?

_____

Wally Can't Do It Alone. He Needs Help.

We all need help sometimes! Who can you ask for help?

If I Invented a New Candy...

What it would look like:

Name: _____

Ingredients: _____

Recipe Steps to Make: _____

Let's Play!

Color and cut. Lay the cards face down. Flip over two cards. If they match, keep the cards! If they don't, flip the cards back over, but don't move them! Try again until all matches are found.

Grandpa Is Happy Wally and Benji Love the Factory Like He Does.

What do you love that is the same as someone in your family?

_____

Mix and Mix and Mix Some More!

What flavor is the candy Peter is mixing?

_____

Dinner Table Chat!

Color and cut out each card. Place one card on each plate during dinner for the person sitting at that spot to read. Or put them all face down in the middle of the table to take turns drawing a new question! Add more by making up your own.

- TELL ME about your favorite family vacation.
- TELL ME one thing you love about each person at this table.
- TELL ME your favorite place to be in your house. Why?
- TELL ME about your favorite part of school.
- JOIN ME by teaching everyone your favorite dance move!
- TELL ME your top 3 favorite candies.
- TELL ME about your first job, or what you want to be when you grow up.
- JOIN ME in acting out your favorite family tradition.
- TELL ME about your favorite Halloween costume.
- JOIN ME by acting out which animal you would want to be.

Let's Do a Puzzle!

Color and cut along the dotted lines to make a puzzle. Have fun trying to put it back together!